ISBN 978-1-9995888-0-9

Written, photographed, illustrated and designed by Joanne Condon.
Edited by Maria Moynihan.

Projects are for recreational purposes only.

Font style, front cover title in Lucky Dip Fernando and Marvellous. Titles and cover pages in Sunset Hill Solid and Marvellous by Aquarius Logos. Font Gill Sans.
Watercolour paint marks created by Lauren Hornaday of PaperEpoch.
Everbuild- A Sika Company sugar soap, Krud Kutter, Harris Brushes from LG Harris & Co Limited.
Colourtrend paints, manufactured in Ireland by General Paints Ltd. Montana Cans made in Germany. Mod Podge is a registered Trade Mark of Plaid Enterprises, Inc. FrogTape is a registered trademark of Shurtape Technologies. Stencils are by www.stencilit.com. Decals are by www.madeofsundays.com, Ronseal is a registered trademark of the Sherwin-Williams Company, Dutch Painter, and Shabby Chic wallpaper is copyright of Pip Studio.

12 COLOUR POPPING PAINTED FURNITURE PROJECTS

FURNITURE CRUSH

BY JOANNE CONDON

To my pledging legends.

Furniture Crush is dedicated to the 156 funders who funded this book through
www.fundit.ie
I want to sincerely thank each and every one of you from the bottom of my heart.

www.jayand.co

FOREWORD

Even though I haven't met Joanne in person YET, we share the same love for painting furniture, using pops of colour while thinking outside of the box. I first noticed Joanne's work on Twitter and from that we sparked up a conversation. This in turn led us to chatting on the telephone about each other's work and our love for something unique and colourful.

You can easily see that Joanne loves what she does and the sense of fun comes out in her work through her unique approach. Her enthusiasm extends to teaching and sharing her passion, both of which I also enjoy. Sharing techniques and creating transformations are what makes revamping furniture so addictive.

Furniture Crush is a great reflection of looking at something that could easily be thrown out and transforming it into something almost unrecognisable. The vibrant colours keep you wanting more, throughout this book. The instructions are easy to follow and everyone will come away with more than enough inspiration and know how to begin tackling their own projects.

As a designer and furniture restorer, I am always on the look-out for inspiring ideas, different approaches and of course having fun. This book has each of these elements in abundance.

Jay Blades,
Founder of Jay&Co, TV presenter

CONTENTS

Introduction

What you are about to embark on is a journey to think outside the box. Reimagine, recreate and reuse something, giving it a whole new lease of life. Not only are you going to have tonnes of fun, you are going to learn lots of useful tricks and fall back in love with old pieces of furniture you may have even considered throwing away!

I have spent years experimenting and looking for the best paint, best technique and easiest ways to get the best finish to make your piece of furniture stand the test of time. The most important element to all the work of transforming a piece of furniture is that you can live with it and not be afraid to use it, clean it and make it a useful part of your home.

How I began

I come from a family of DIYers and makers. Growing up, we knitted, we drew, we painted, we mended and we created. I always wanted to do something in the art world. I attended art college and received a degree in fine art. I became an art teacher and studied art education for teachers.

As I was training to be an art teacher, myself and my now husband were also building our home and I wanted everything in the house to be full of character and personality. It was so difficult to find furniture that I loved, so I started up-cycling old pieces my family had stored in the garage.

Teaching was one of my first passions, but I qualified right at the height of the recession. It was difficult to get a full-time job where I could feel secure and grow with my work. So I decided to create my own job, doing exactly what I loved.

I have painted furniture for many years and I opened up my business, Kyle Lane, in November 2011. Kyle Lane is the biggest passion for me. I have been painting furniture, teaching workshops and am now writing this book to share all that I have learned through my years of painting furniture in my studio and at home, every single day.

I am obsessed with old furniture: painting it, giving it a whole new lease of life and experimenting and using different techniques to create pieces that you can't stop thinking about and grow the biggest crush on.

Are you ready to fall back in love with that piece of old furniture?

Then turn that page…

TOOLS

There are three main places where I get my supplies:

1. A hardware store
2. A building supplies store
3. An art/craft supplies shop

These have the basics and usually if one shop doesn't have a particular item I am looking for, the next one will.

Wallpaper and fabrics can be sourced at a good interiors shop and for anything you can't find in the three places above, you most certainly will locate it online.

I would invest in a good sander to take time and effort off the preparation stage.

Good quality paint brushes make all the difference, as well as the quality of the paint. Buying cheaper versions of these will definitely hamper the quality of your finish.

Here is a list of the most common tools I use every day and throughout this book:

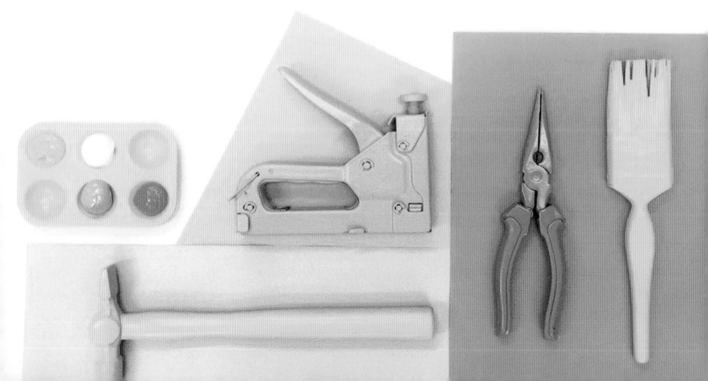

SUGAR SOAP

KRUD KUTTER

MASK

PROTECTIVE GLASSES

GLOVES

SANDING BLOCKS

CIRCULAR SANDER

SANDING DISKS

PAINT BRUSHES

Recommended: *Everbuild Sugarsoap, Krud Kutter, Harris Brushes.*
Credit: geometric nails by Nicola at www.blush.ie

13

FOAM ROLLER

ARTIST BRUSHES

KID'S PAINT BRUSH

PRIMER

UNDERCOAT

SATIN WOOD/LATEX PAINT

SPRAY PAINT

CLEAR VARNISH

MOD PODGE

Recommended: *Colourtrend Primer, Undercoat and Satin. Montana Cans Spray Paint. Ronseal Satin Clear Varnish. Mod Podge glue and adhesive.*

FROGTAPE

WALLPAPER

CRAFTER'S KNIFE

GOLD LEAF

CARBON PAPER

STENCILS

HAMMER

STAPLE REMOVER

STAPLER

Recommended: *FrogTape. Stencils from Stencil It.*

furniture crush

(n) to develop a strong desire for a piece of furniture.
Especially if it is painted, revamped, upcycled, recreated, enhanced or reimagined.

Colour
Is
Everything

#furniturecrush

Getting Started

Enjoy painting: it's one of the most relaxing things and it's not a time for stress.
If it goes wrong, it's ok. You can always paint over it. If it's your first time painting, don't rush it. Take your time and enjoy it and don't be worrying. This is fun and worrying about messing it up before you even start is going to suck all the enjoyment out of it. If it's not going to plan, take a step back, look at it and evaluate what might be going wrong and how you can fix it. It's a great learning process. This book is going to help.

Planning

I always like to look at the piece of furniture and let it "talk to me". I look at the era it was made in and the style that was popular at that time. I see if it is something that interests me, and draw inspiration from the colours and patterns of that period.

The best way to have a full blown crush on your furniture is to plan it properly and paint it correctly so it will stand the wear and tear of everyday life.

Colour

If you have a piece of furniture you are just dying to paint, grabbing the first tin you have may not be the best move. Colour is EVERYTHING. Trust me. It's the difference between loving something and liking something, and if you are going to all that effort of painting, you want to make sure it's going to be a piece you love!

Look at the colour on your walls and décor. You don't want to paint your piece the same shade of cream if it's going on a cream carpet or against a cream wall; you might not be able to even see it. You can go neutral or bold- it's your choice- but let the room "talk to you".

For example, you can pull colours from textiles in your room, like curtains that you won't be getting rid of anytime soon. And even if you do discard them down the line, you can always change the paint colour.

If you already have pieces of furniture at home you can work on, or pieces in your shed, then you can get started right away. If you don't, then take a look at sourcing on the next section.

Sourcing

But where do you find all this furniture if you have none to start off with?

If it's the very beginning of your furniture painting journey, have a look in your garage for something small to experiment with. You don't want your very first project to be a big kitchen dresser that has been in your family for years and stands in the main area of your home for everyone to see. Taking a small item will give you the confidence to tackle a bigger project.

Second hand furniture shops are far easier to find these days than in the past. Some charities may have a dedicated shop just for furniture, so the best way to find out is to ask. Check out car boot sales, auctions, flea markets and online sellers.

WHAT TO
look out FOR

PRICE

Prices really differ depending on where you buy your old furniture, so there is no real guide as to what you should spend. If I thought a piece of furniture was perfect for what I had in mind, however, I would be willing to spend more money on the piece.

Don't be distracted by low prices. If a chair is really cheap, but is really damaged or has a leg falling off, you may have to hire someone to fix it, which will cost you more money and time.

Low Price

STRUCTURE

If the piece is really wobbly, you may have to hire someone to fix it for you, so that should be considered. Check all areas of the piece you are buying. If it has drawers, take them out and have a closer look. Look at the back panels and underneath if possible.

Things to look out for are wood rot and woodworm. Woodworm can of course be treated, but always do so before you bring it into your home. (Find out more about woodworm on page 122.)

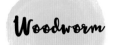

Woodworm

Top Tip: To get a closer look at the condition of a piece of furniture, you can use the light on your phone to take a look at the darker areas.

Plan

Sketching out your ideas for your piece of furniture before you start helps you to visualise what your piece might look like and get all your ideas out on paper. It doesn't have to be a work of art, just a quick sketch to get those creative juices flowing.

Preparation

When it comes to durability of furniture, preparation is key. You need to be able to live with your furniture. You want to be able to wipe your furniture clean easily and without a second thought. You don't want to be worrying about damaging it. If you are going to go through painting it, quick results will cost you in the long run. Not preparing your piece after going through all the bother of painting it will only lead to frustration unless you never touch it.

Clean It

Cleaning with sugar soap

Wiping away residue

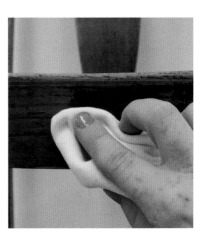

Cleaning with Krud Kutter

To prepare, ALWAYS clean down the surface. I use sugar soap. I always use a spray bottle as it is convenient and easy to use. Wear gloves as there are chemicals in this product and it's a great cleaner to get rid of dirt and grime that can build up on old furniture. Spray the surface and leave sit for a minute to work into the dirt. With a slightly dampened cloth wipe down the piece to make sure you don't have any sugar soap residue.

For extra greasy surfaces, Krud Kutter is a great product to remove stubborn grime.

Always turn the piece upside down and clean away any cobwebs or dirt that has gathered underneath. I clean everything first, even if it looks like it doesn't need it. Trust me, don't skip this step. It dries really quickly, so you don't have to wait too long before you go onto the next step.

Sand it

Sanding is the best way to ensure that your primer or undercoat will stick and stay on your piece of furniture. This is where your durability comes in. Once you have a well prepared surface, it will stand up to everyday wear and tear. I use a sanding block (medium grit) on smaller pieces as it's easy to hold and control and can get into awkward areas, especially spindles on chairs.

What grit sandpapers to use and what are the different grades for?
Coarse Sandpaper: 80 grit sandpaper for removing finish on furniture i.e. varnish.
Medium Sandpaper: 120 grit sandpaper for preparing surface for painting.
Fine Sandpaper: 220 grit for sanding in between coats of paint for smooth finish.

Always sand in the direction of the grain. This is to avoid scratching the surface and creating visible scratch lines.

Sand awkward areas first with a
medium sanding block.

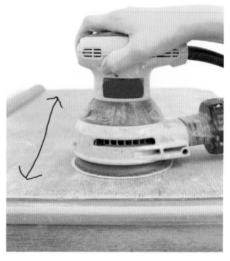

Sanding larger areas with a
circular sander.

If you're using a sander, even a circular sander, always go in the direction of the grain of the timber, getting all the harder-to-reach areas with a sanding block first and then the larger areas with the larger sander. If you sand awkward areas with an electric sander, you risk damaging or removing areas you don't want to as it can be powerful and harder to control.

After sanding, you need to remove the dust from the piece of furniture, which you can do with the brush attachment with the hoover.

If you don't have this attachment, use a large fence paint brush, regularly dusting the brush with your hand to ensure no dust goes back onto the piece of furniture. This is only to get rid of the large dust particles. You will then need to give it a rub with a dry cloth i.e. cheese cloth.

Removing the majority of the dust with the brush hoover attachment.

Wiping remaining dust with a dry cloth.

NB: Make sure your piece of furniture and the surface you're painting on is completely dust free before you start painting.

Hinges and Hardware

If you can't remove the hinges or the hardware, make sure you protect them from the paint. Wrapping them in FrogTape, covering them in Vaseline or wrapping them in tinfoil are ways to protect the metal before you start painting. I like to use a small, flat artist's brush to paint around the hinges as well.

Covering hardware in FrogTape.

Painting around hinges.

Prepare for painting

Depending on the surface, it will need to be prepared with undercoat or a primer coat or both. Here is how to distinguish which method to use.

When to prime: Primer is a great product and has many uses. You use a primer when the surface has never been treated e.g. like bare timber. It can also be used as a stain block and as an adhesive with a difficult surface that is being painted, like veneer or a highly shiny surface. Primer can also be used to cover knots in the timber.

You can also use a good primer as a basecoat when you are painting PVC. Yes, you can paint PVC with a layer of primer and then go in with your Satinwood, just like you are painting any piece.

When to undercoat: You use undercoat after a primer, or when you are painting over a surface that has already been painted.

If you use a coat of primer, then use one coat of undercoat. If you are using only undercoat, use two coats.

Primers: Bare surface, difficult surface or stain block.
Undercoat: When the surface has already been painted or primed.

When prepping your piece of furniture with undercoat/primer, paint all the awkward areas first. If you are painting a chair or anything small, you can turn it over and paint everything you see first.

Paint all awkward areas with a brush.

I use a roller usually only on large pieces, like a wardrobe, or when there is a large surface area to cover after I have painted all the awkward areas with a brush.

Some paint colours that have a really high pigment e.g. dark or deep colours, need an undercoat with a tint of colour in it. For example, yellow can be a really difficult paint colour for coverage and you will always need more coats of paint. Using a light grey tint in the undercoat can help with this.

Preparing Drawers

Drawers may present some challenges when preparing them. Let's look at some of the common problems and how to make sure they don't cause issues later.

When taking out the drawers, number them in order with some chalk on the underside.

On the piece of furniture, line the inside of where the drawer inserts into the piece with FrogTape. This is to ensure that the drawers don't get stuck as you try and put them back in and also allows for a more crisp looking finish.

If you have lots of wiggle room between your drawer and the side edge of your piece you can paper or paint them. If they are tight, painting the sides could mean you may have a lot of difficulty in trying to get them to fit back in again so please be aware of this.

Tape off the front section with
FrogTape for a clean line.

Prepare and paint the edge of the
drawer like normal.

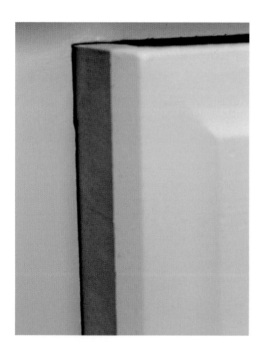

This drawer is an example of a
drawer with little wiggle room.
Painting the sides would make them
very difficult to close. Rubbing a
clear furniture wax into the edges
will help with movement.

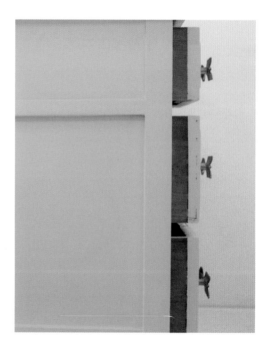

What the finished drawers will look
like when opened, once they are
painted. Nice and neat.

Using Wood Filler

Drawers can get a lot of wear and tear. If an area of the drawer has a chip of wood missing you can easily cover this up. This method can be used on any trouble spot/area, not just the drawers.

Look carefully at the chip. If it is lifting it may need to be glued down with wood glue. If a small chip is very loose, you can carefully remove it.

With a scraper, fill the hole with wood filler. Dipping the top of the scraper in a small amount of water can help the scraper move more easily across the filler area.

Fill any area that has a chip or dip and scrape the sides using the edge of the drawer to lean on. Leave to fully dry (overnight is best).

Sand off the wood filler until it is flush with surrounding timber.

Once it is flush with the rest of the surface, use fine paper to make the surface smooth and clean with a dry cloth.

Prepare your surface like normal.

Painting

I always like to leave the primer/undercoat layer rest and fully dry out at least 24 hours before I start with the first coat of paint. It's rare that I would prime/undercoat and give two coats of paint all in the one day.

Before painting, take a look at your piece. If there are any lumps or bumps, you can sand them down with sandpaper and brush away any dust before painting.

What type of paint to use?

There are lots of different types of paint on the market now, and it can be very confusing as to which brand to use.

I love experimenting with new products, but in my opinion you can't beat the durability and finish of a traditional Satinwood paint. It stands the test of time, is so easy to live with and once you're finished painting, it doesn't discolour. Also, you don't need to add another layer and when you're finished painting, it's done.

There are also many brands of Satinwood available at different price points, but in my experience the cheaper you go, the more watery the consistency of paint, the more coats you need, the more work you need to do and after all that, the more discolouration over time will occur. So quality and brand are top of my list when choosing paint. I like a good quality paint at a reasonable price point, which has a good consistency and doesn't discolour over time.

My advice is no matter what paint you're using, always prepare the surface well and it will be more durable.

Things to look out for

Water based and low VOC. In every product that I use, I always try and go for the water based. It's easier to work with, clean after use and better for the environment.

Low VOC is also very important. Low VOC refers to volatile organic compounds that are not harmful to the environment and humans. It mostly refers to paints and other products that have a very low or zero VOC, e.g. sealants, adhesives and cleaners.

Your paint brush should never be dripping with paint. Make sure when you dip your paint brush in tin that you remove all the extra paint on the side. If you put too much paint in your brush, you tend to create a little pool that you continually drag your brush back into. As a result, the paint underneath that pool will start to dry as you drag it out and you will be spreading paint that is dry onto paint that is wet, leading to an uneven finish.

Scraping paint brush off the edge of the tin to ensure you don't have too much paint on your brush.

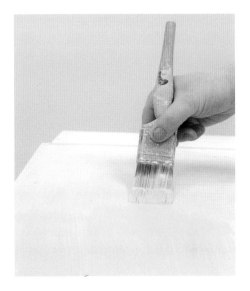

When painting, keep your hand down close to the stainless steel part of the brush to help you keep more control of the brush.

Don't worry after your first coat of paint if you think it's not as beautiful as you had imagined in your head. Every piece goes through an "ugly phase". Once you have the second coat of paint on and you start pulling your piece together, it's going to be fabulous.

With a paint brush, paint all awkward areas first, just like when you are undercoating.

For larger pieces of furniture you can get great coverage with a roller. Leave to fully dry.

Repeat the steps for a second coat of paint.

For an overall smooth finish, sand in between coats with a fine sandpaper, leaving adequate drying time between each coat.

For smaller items, turn them upside down and paint all the awkward areas first.

Please note: Some colours are harder for coverage e.g. high pigment colours like yellow or red.

For really deep colours like charcoal grey and bottle-green navy, you can get the undercoat mixed in a shade of the colour.

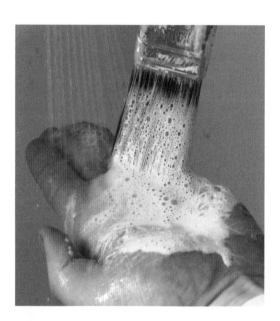

Brush care: To keep your brushes clean and lasting longer at the end of the day I like to wash out any residue of paint. Put a little pea size amount of an eco friendly washing up liquid and lather it up in the palm of your hand and rinse really well.

If you leave your paint brush out overnight by mistake, don't throw it away. You can still save it. Leave the bristles of the brush soak in fabric conditioner for 24 hours. The fabric conditioner breaks down the paint and you can rinse it off. Your brush will also smell pretty- bonus!

I can not stop looking at you!

I can not stop looking at you!

I can not stop looking at you!

#furniturecrush

And there you were...

Light Upholstery

TECHNIQUE

Take A Seat

LIGHT UPHOLSTERY TECHNIQUE

Chairs are one of the easiest things to come across and make a great starter project for a newbie. Kitchen chairs can last for decades, but updating them can keep you on trend. A new fabric change can transform the whole look of your kitchen.

BEFORE

THIS IS A FUN WEEKEND PROJECT AND IT'S A GREAT WAY TO BRIGHTEN UP A CORNER IN ANY ROOM.

Plan

create colour block

Pull Blue from fabric

Retro Fabric (Bold colours)

MATERIALS REQUIRED

Undercoat
Satinwood paint (I used
Coloutrend satin in Milk Teeth and
Enchanted Evening)
Staple remover
Staple gun and staples
Wadding
Fabric
Scissors
Fire Resistant Lining
Eye protective glasses

Method

When painting the chair, it is best practice to paint it first upside down, painting everything you see, and then turn it the right way around and paint everything else that you missed.

Remove the seat pad from the chair. It may just be a pop-in pad that you can remove or it could be screwed onto the chair.

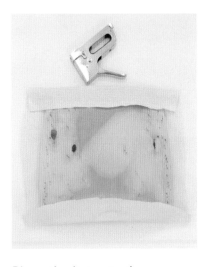

Wearing protective eyewear, remove the seat pad from the chair with a staple remover. Push the staple remover underneath the staple.

Pry out the staple. Cut your new piece of fabric and lining, making sure you have an inch around each side to pull and staple. If your foam is a little flat, you can add a layer of wadding.

Place the lining in the correct position and staple onto your seat, stapling the middle parts of the top and bottom first.

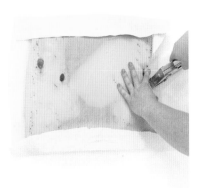

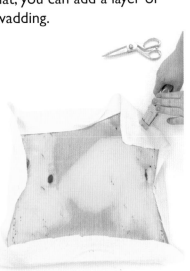

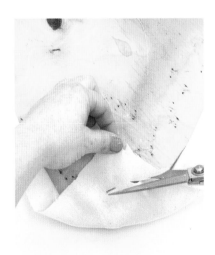

You will need to pull the fabric (not too tight) so that it is comfortably stretched. Follow this by pulling the fabric and stapling the middle of the sides.

Working on the corner is the key to a neat finish. Pull the corner of the fabric diagonally opposite the corner.

Cut the extra piece of fabric (it will look like a mini triangle) and staple directly opposite that corner.

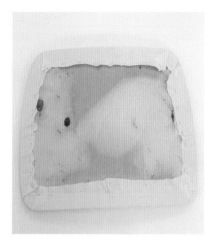

Once that is cut away, fold in the right side of the corner and staple, followed by the left side of that corner and staple. This allows for a neat corner.

Work on the next corner directly opposite the corner you have just stapled. This is to ensure a nice and neat stretch of the fabric over the chair.

Complete the other set of corners and staple the whole way around the seat pad to the areas in between.

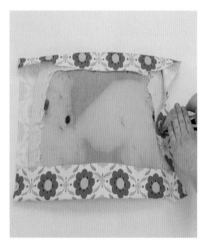

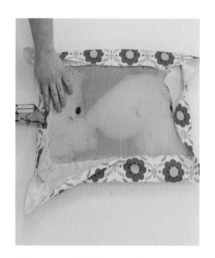

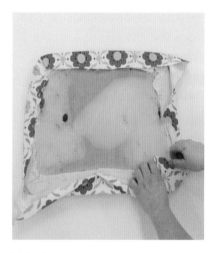

Repeat the same process for your chosen fabric. Staple the top and bottom first.

Then staple from side to side, making sure you are stretching it a little, so that it's not too tight but not too loose, and then the corners diagonally.

Working in this sequence ensures that the fabric is stretched evenly and neatly.

Top Tip   Use the old piece of the fabric as a template for your new piece of fabric.

Like before, after you have put the staple directly on the corner, remove the extra piece of fabric at that corner.

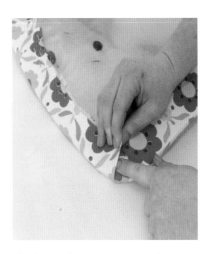

Tuck in the corner at the right side of the staple and at the left side of the staple.

Once you have completed all corners, work your way around the chair, comfortably stretching each section and securing with a staple.

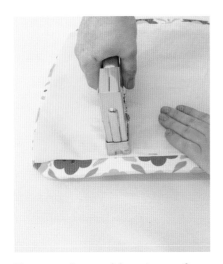

To complete, add a piece of lining to the back of the seat pad, folding in the edges and stapling in position.

Staple all the way around. Place the seat pad back on the chair (the same way you removed it).

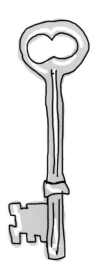

The corners are key so spend some extra time to make sure you have them set up properly.

Applying Wallpaper

Paper Perfect

APPLYING WALLPAPER TECHNIQUE

This is a really good way to get a completely different look and add pops of colour into a piece. Applying feature wallpaper can really add value, and lining the inside of the drawers can be a nice surprise.

BEFORE

WALLPAPERING THE INSIDE OF THE DRAWER CAN REALLY ADD A GREAT FINISH TO A PROJECT. YOU CAN USE UP SOME WALLPAPER FROM A PREVIOUS PROJECT OR SPLURGE ON A REAL SHOW STOPPER.

Plan

Keep Old handles

Flower Wallpaper

Paint Rim

Satinwood Overall Lady Nicole

MATERIALS REQUIRED

Good quality wallpaper (I used
Pip Studio wallpaper
Sandpaper and Undercoat
Satinwood Paint (I used Colourtrend
Lady Nicole)
Paint brushes
Furniture Mod Podge
Craft blade
Scissors
Sponge
Steel ruler
Chalk

Method

Lay out the drawers in order. I always write the number sequence underneath the drawer in chalk to make sure I keep them in that order. If there are handles, remove them at this stage.

Plan where you are going to place the wallpaper, but do not paint these areas in Satinwood as the wallpaper won't stick to that surface properly. However, you should sand and undercoat them.
(If you are using a light paper, skipping this step may result in some of the timber/stains peeping through.)

Sand, undercoat and paint the rest of the piece in Satinwood. Line up the drawers in the order in which they will be placed in the piece. Use the numbers on the back to guide you.

I had a little rim on the drawer fronts that will be seen, so I painted these in the same Satinwood colour as the rest of the locker.

Taking a length of your wallpaper in your hand, use your thumb and index finger to press about the edges of the paper to get a crease guide to the placement of the drawers.

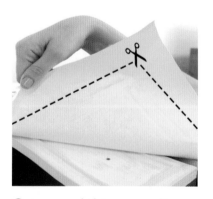

Cut around this crease line, but not directly on it. You should leave an extra bit of paper if possible to allow for some wiggle room. You can always cut any extra paper away later.

Top Tip

If you are using wallpaper on a table top, get a glass top cut to protect the paper.

With a brush, apply Mod Podge onto the wallpaper in an even coat: not too thick, as this may cause bubbling, but enough to cover the paper. The paper will expand a little, so make sure you leave it settle. Just when you can see the glue beginning to soak in, it's ready to apply.

Apply the paper from left to right, section by section, with the palm of your hand or with a dry sponge, applying a little pressure to push out any air bubbles. Smooth out the paper until you reach the end of the drawer

With a sharp craft blade, carefully cut away the extra paper, using the ruler as your guide. Cut in short motions, as running the blade along the paper will result in it ripping and tearing.

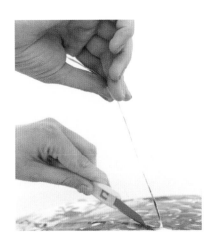

Top Tip

To give you better visability on what line you are cutting, hold back the section that you have just cut.

To prevent the paper from tearing when you re-attach the handles, pierce a little hole with the blade to help the handle go back through easily.

If your paper is ripping, make sure the blade is nice and sharp and not one that has been used a lot. A new craft blade can make all the difference.

Handmade teddy by www.daintydressdiaries.com
Wallpaper in Dutch Painter White from www.pipstudio.com

Changing Handles

You Can Handle It

CHANGING HANDLES TECHNIQUE

Sometimes falling in love with handles that don't fit your furniture can be a bad thing. But here is the solution. You can change your handles anytime with this little filler trick. Change one bolt hole to two, or change two to one. The choice is yours. Updating the handles can also lift a piece of furniture even if you are not painting it.

BEFORE

THIS OFFICE DESK ORIGINALLY HAD A MIRROR ON IT WHICH WAS USED AS A VANITY, THESE CAN ALWAYS BE EASILY REMOVED!

Plan

Bright Colour maybe Turquoise

Change handles

Polish wheels

Wallpaper Inside drawers

MATERIALS REQUIRED

Undercoat
Satin paint (I used Colourtrend Island Breeze)
Drill and drill bit (same size as your new handle fitting)
Wood filler
Painter's tool/filler tool
Sanding sponge
New handles
Pencil
Measuring tape/ruler

Remove the old handle from the drawer. It doesn't matter what holes the old handles have left behind as they can be easily filled.

Using your finger, push the wood filler in to fill the old holes and pat down with your finger gently, making sure that you have completely filled the hole.

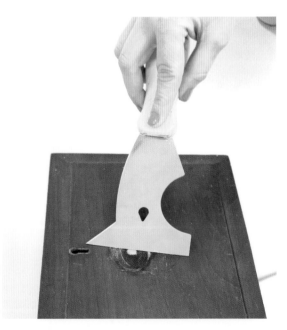

Scrape across the drawer with a scraper to remove any excess filler. You can dip the scraper tip into a bit of water beforehand to help it drag across smoothly. Leave until fully dry (overnight). Sand back the wood filler until it becomes flush with the drawer.

Prepare and prime your piece (refer to page 26).
Carefully measure your drawer and position the handles correctly. Mark out the new holes for your new handle.

Using a drill piece the same thickness as the bar on your new handles, drill the new hole, following your guide mark.

Paint your piece like on page 31.
Add your new hardware onto your painted piece and secure the back of the handle with the appropriate fittings.

Sometimes old handles can be given a new lease of life by spraying them or painting them.

Wallpapering the inside drawer can also be a lovely addition to a project.

Top Tip

**MEASURE TWICE,
DRILL ONCE.**

WHEN I WAKE UP

in the morning,

I RUN TO

see you first.

#furniturecrush

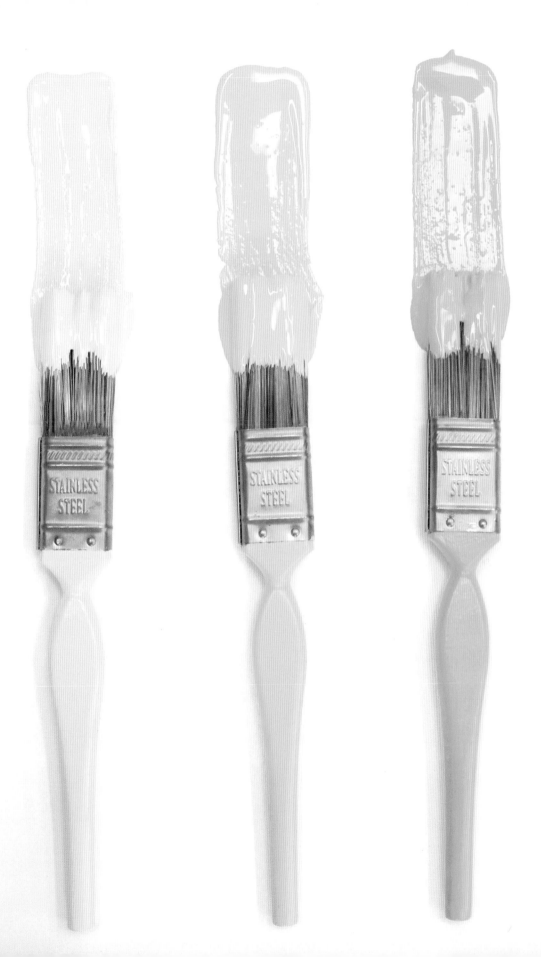

White Wash and Distressed

TECHNIQUE

The Heart Of The Kitchen

WHITE WASH AND DISTRESSING TECHNIQUE

The dresser is the heart and soul of the kitchen. It is where we display our wares and we can really get a feel for someone's taste by revealing what they exhibit! So you need to make it a show stopper.

BEFORE

PAINTING PLAIN WOODEN HANDLES CAN BE JUST AS EFFECTIVE AS BUYING EXPENSIVE ONES. YOU CAN PAINT POLKA DOT, STRIPES OR SOME DETAIL TO MAKE THEM STAND OUT.

Plan

White wash top

Spray handles white

White Back Panel

white handles

Plain white handles

Distress areas that would get worn naturally.

MATERIALS REQUIRED

Undercoat
Satinwood Paint
(I used Colourtrend satin
in Egg Blue and Milk Teeth)
Paintbrush
Sander and sanding disks in 80 grit,
120 and 220
Sanding block
Mask
Cloth or sponge
Clear varnish
FrogTape
Hoover

Method

You will need a circular sander for this technique, as sanding the top section by hand would be too time consuming. Use 80 (medium grade) grit sandpaper disk, 120 (fine grade) grit sandpaper disk and 220 sandpaper disk (extra fine).

Before you paint your dresser in your desired colour, you must first tackle the area that you want to white wash; in this project, the top section.

To prepare your chosen area for white washing, you must first sand back the surface. Wearing a mask in a well ventilated area, sand back the top section of the dresser using a medium grit sandpaper (80 grit) with your sander. Always go in the direction of the grain of the timber.

Sand until the varnish is completely removed. Sand again with a finer sandpaper (120 grit) to smooth the area. It is really important to remove all varnish and finish on this step so that the timber is completely bare. If you leave any residue of varnish, the white wash will not soak into the timber as intended. Hoover and dust off any dust and clean the top of the dresser with a dry cloth to make sure all the dust is removed.

Top Tip Only distress areas where the dresser would naturally get worn (i.e. under where a drawer handle would get pulled, the corners where it would get shabby).

White washing is an easy way to lift the dresser, but also keep the most used area durable for the heavy wear and tear it will receive. Water down white Satinwood paint 3 parts paint to 1 part water. Mix the paint/water mixture really well. Paint on the watery paint on to the surface in sections.

Rub it in with a cloth or a sponge and really work and buff into the grain. Only do section by section to ensure an even coat of white wash on the surface. Work with the grain of the timber. Seal with 4-5 thin layers of clear varnish, leaving to fully dry in between each coat and buffing with 220 sandpaper.

Paint the dresser. I went for a two tone colour. After I painted the piece overall, I painted the back section white. This will require steady hands to cut in with the paint along the line where the two colours meet. If you are having difficulty, you can tape the painted section with FrogTape to allow for a sharper line.

For the distressed look, use a sanding block to sand the edges of the dresser in areas you think would get worn and most use, lightly at first and then at the edges. Work your way up to the desired look.

Spraying Wicker

TECHNIQUE

Sad Wicker To Heart Flicker

SPRAYING WICKER TECHNIQUE

Wicker can really be transformed when some colour is added. These chairs are also relatively cheap to pick up and I always come across them easily. There are many different styles and shapes available and they are quite comfortable to sit on.

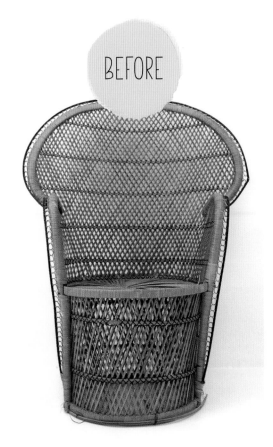

BEFORE

ADD POPS OF COLOUR WITH ACCESSORIES LIKE WOOL POM POMS AND A FUNKY CUSHION. THEY CAN BE REAL GEMS IN ANY ROOM.

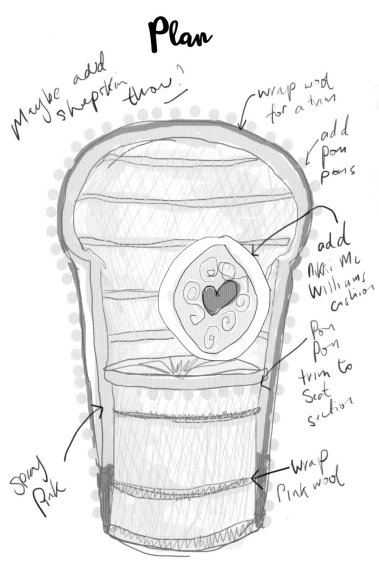

Plan

Maybe add sheepskin throw!

wrap wool for a trim

add pom poms

add Nikki Mc Williams cushion

Pom Pom trim to seat section

Spray Pink

Wrap Pink wool

MATERIALS REQUIRED

Dry brush
Mask
Wicker chair
1 x spray can of primer
(I used Montana Primer)
2-3 x spray cans of paint
(I used Montana GOLD in Lychee 3000)
Hoover brush attachment
Wool/pom poms and
 glue gun (optional)

Method

Start by cleaning the inside base of the chair, with a dry brush in the direction of the straw to get rid of all the extra dust and build up of grime. Work your way around the chair.

With a Hoover brush attachment, now vacuum up all the extra dust all the way around the chair.

Priming is a step that is not to be skipped! It is key to a vibrant overall colour and also makes it more durable. Shake the can for a full five minutes before you break the seal.

Starting on the inside of the base, spray with the primer going over and back in fluid motions, slightly overlapping the spray on each line.

Work your way around the chair, making sure you hit every spot that you can. Leave to fully dry.

Once again, shake the can of paint for a full five minutes before you break the seal. Starting on the inside, spray in the direction of the wicker lengths, catching the diagonal straws on the way around.

Top Tip Always wear a mask when using spray and make sure you are in a well ventilated area. Also make sure to spend extra time on cleaning to guarantee a good overall finish.

Don't over spray, as this will lead to dribbling. Spray evenly around the whole chair for its first coat. Leave to fully dry.

Spray the second coat and cover any areas that you have missed. Turn the chair upside down to make sure you haven't missed any areas.

Hide any damaged areas by wrapping threads/wool and creating a whole new look by adding other elements of wool and pom poms. I added the pom poms in a similar colour to the spray paint by applying them with a glue gun.

Wrap a stronger pink wool in a crisscross stitch with a large needle. You can add different colour wool if you like.

Cushion by www.nikkimcwilliams.com

I can't wait
to see what
you look like

#furniturecrush

Geometric

TECHNIQUE

Geometric-ness is Best

PAINTING GEOMETRIC TECHNIQUE

This project may need a little extra time, but trust me, it will be worth it in the end. It's a great way to pop colour into a piece of furniture, and even one triangle in a corner can give you a whole new look.

FrogTape is really the best tape for this type of project. It will not remove the paint layer underneath, nor will the paint seep underneath the edges. Make sure your brush isn't loaded with water before you start.

BEFORE

YOU CAN ALSO PAINT YOUR PIECE ALL OVER IN ONE COLOUR FIRST, TAPE THE TRIANGLES WITH THE FROGTAPE AND PAINT. THIS TAKES LESS TIME AND IS EQUALLY AS EFFECTIVE.

MATERIALS REQUIRED

Undercoat
Satinwood paint
(I used Colourtrend satin in Island Breeze, Purple Holyhock, Pink Explosion, Wildflower Boutique, Pale Petunia, Happy Face, Blue Bliss and Cyan Sky)
FrogTape
Paintbrush
Measuring tape(optional)

Plan

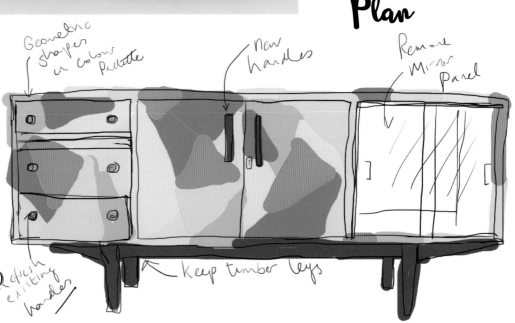

Geometric shapes in colour palette

New handles

Remove Mirror Panel

Refinish existing handles

Keep timber legs

Method

After you have prepared and undercoated your piece, make a quick sketch to plan your overall geometric look to guide the approximate size of the triangles you may use, as in the example above.

It doesn't have to be perfect, but getting an idea of how you want to arrange the colours will put your mind at ease. You could use a ruler and make this really precise, but that may take all the fun out of it. After your first set of triangles are complete, work off these triangles every time. Make triangles out of every shape left. There may be some larger triangles and some smaller ones, but that's ok: it will all come together in the end. Trust me.

In this project the secret is using FrogTape. FrogTape will save you a lot of time afterwards, it has a magic ingredient that enables you to keep paint out and keep your lines sharp. I know what's not to love! I used FrogTape painter's multi-surface as I left adequate drying time in between coats. If you have less time I would suggest using FrogTape painter's delicate surface (yellow tape).

Working from the plan, begin with the first layer of triangles, making sure that each piece of the tape is firmly in place.

Use your fingers to run along the edge of the tape to make sure it is fully stuck to the surface.

Now it is time to start painting your triangles. Don't go too heavy on the paint or you will be left with a thick edge line. Gently peel back the FrogTape straight away (leaving the tape on until the paint is dry may cause surface damage). Leave that triangle until fully dry.

Top Tip

Make sure that each edge of the FrogTape is firmly in place before you paint and that you remove the FrogTape immediately after painting to prevent damage to the surface.

Once the first layer of paint is completely dry, add the next layer of triangular shapes over the edges of the dry ones to create a seamless line between the two.

Paint in the next colour of your choice. Peel back the FrogTape immediately and then leave the paint to fully dry.

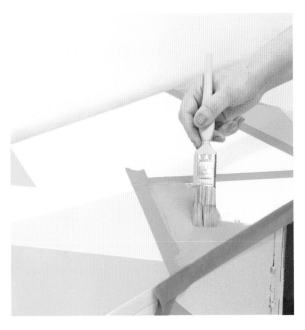

Keep repeating this process until you have the areas covered in the colours you have chosen.

Gently peel back the FrogTape in between each layer immediately after your finished painting. Add the next and final layer of triangular shapes to your piece.

In this piece, I also changed the two handles on the centre doors, as well as their position, as seen on page 48.

Home Sweet Home sign from www.cottonclara.com | Handles from Sarah Beeny Home | Girl Prints by
www.racheljpowell.com | Other prints from www.eastendprints.co.uk

Ombré

TECHNIQUE

Outstanding Ombré

PAINTING OMBRE TECHNIQUE

This is the ultimate show-stopping buffet side table. These pieces are one of the most useful and stylish pieces of storage you could own.

BEFORE

DRESS IT UP FOR A PARTY, USE IT AS AN ENTRY PIECE IN A HALLWAY OR EVEN AS A CHANGING TABLE IN NURSERY.

MATERIALS REQUIRED

Undercoat
Selection of brushes
Ruler
Pencil
Satinwood paint in
 a palette of shades.
(I used Colourtrend
satin in
Aromatic Breeze,
Wildflower Boutique,
Cherished One and
Pink Explosion)

Plan

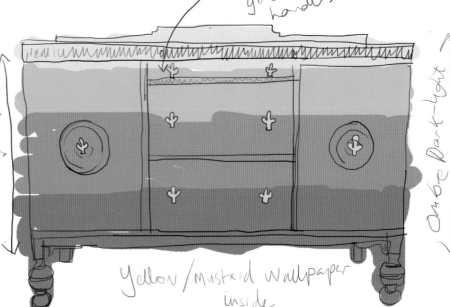

funky gold handles

Blend between colours

Ombre Dark-light

Yellow/Mustard wallpaper inside

Method

Start by painting all of the bottom quarter of this project in dark pink on all four sides. If you want to create a guide to make sure that each quarter is even, you can do so by using a ruler and a little pencil line or paint mark around the piece.

This project is all about building up the colour slowly and making the transition of shades from light to dark blend evenly. Paint the next section in the next lightest shade.

Just apply one coat of each colour and don't worry about creating a perfect line. You will be blending these colours in the next coat.

Finish off the last quarter with the lightest shade of pink. Paint the very top (i.e. the flat top of the sideboard) in the lightest colour (Aromatic Breeze). Leave to fully dry.

Begin your second coat. Paint your darker pink quarter just like before on all four sides. With the second colour, start at the top of that section and paint downwards to meet the quarter below, dragging the brush across the joining.

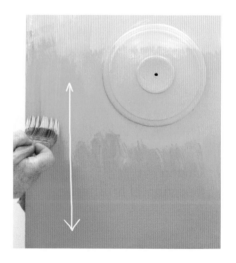

Then immediately after, drag your brush up and down on the joining line. Only do this on the joining line; don't drag the darker colour up to the top of the lighter colour.

Continue this step the whole way up each quarter of your project.

You can leave the very top (i.e. the flat top of the sideboard) of your project in the lightest shade of Aromatic Breeze to give you time to blend the other colours properly.

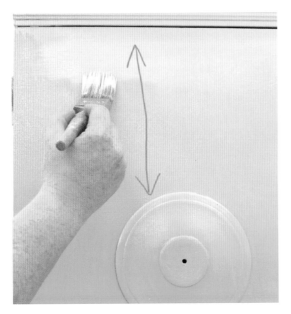

When blending, I kept a separate brush for each of the three joining sections. Starting at the bottom layer again, continue your brushstrokes, this time blending them in all different directions to make sure you have each part blended correctly.

Continue this blending action until you no longer have a definite line on any of the colours. If you need to add more paint, just use a small amount and blend it into a section to lighten or darken that area.

Continue this step until you have every colour blended and buffed to give it a beautiful ombré look. I finished off by giving the very top a second coat of Aromatic Breeze and adding some new handles.

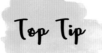

Top Tip Really work in the brushes for the blended areas, and blend, blend, blend.

On the inside of this project, I added a different colour and also wallpapered the inside of the drawers and sides using the applying wallpaper technique in project two.

Amazing light fixtures from www.gwennieslab.nl | Inside drawer Fayre's Fair Wallpaper from www.minimoderns.com

#furniturecrush

YOU HAD ME AT..........

MID-CENTURY LEGS

FreeStyle Painting Pattern

TECHNIQUE

Happy Hour

APPLYING PATTERN FREESTYLE

Using this technique lets your creativity run wild, with lots of patterns to experiment with. It's all about having fun. Dress it up anyway you want, and close it when you're back to your daily life.

BEFORE

WHY NOT HAVE A LITTLE AREA IN YOUR HOUSE WHERE YOU CAN ENTERTAIN GUESTS. IT CAN BE GREAT AS WELL FOR ANY KIND OF A PARTY AS A FOCAL POINT.

Plan

Spray old handles

Polka dots ♡

Continue Pattern all the way around!

80's VIBE

Play with Patterns

Use Decals

Use Vibrant Colours and don't be sorry

Have! Fun!

MATERIALS NEEDED

Satinwood paint
(I used Colourtrend satin in Turkish Teal, Andes Sky, Tartlet, Happy Place, Egg Blue, Wildflower Boutique)
Paint brush
FrogTape
Artist's paint brushes
Rubber from pencil top
Decals from www.madeofsundays.com
Card and scissors

Method

Start by painting a guide line to create your colour section for the first layer of your pattern, then paint in the colour blocks.

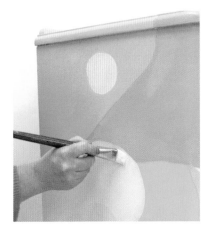

On the second coat, concentrate on getting a sharp line in between the colours with a flat artist's paint brush.

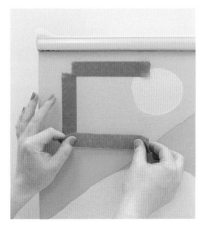

Mark a square section off with FrogTape. You can overlap the shapes to make it more interesting.

Place the top of the pencil rubber in a little bit of paint and dab it onto the piece to create a polka dot.

Start in the middle, creating a line of polka dots, and then staggering the second row in the center. You can also use a ruler and a pencil line to get ¯n accurate pattern.

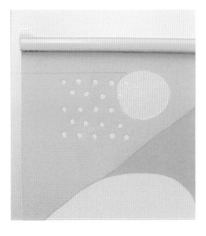

Remove the FrogTape when finished.

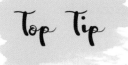

Top Tip If you create a pattern that you don't like, remove the paint with a baby wipe before it dries.

Freestyle some circles with an artist's brush with Satinwood paint.

You will need to give the circles two coats to stand out. Make sure to leave the paint to dry in between each coat.

Make a quick stencil by drawing a circle shape onto a piece of card and cut it out with a scissors.

Secure in place with FrogTape. Paint freestyle lines vertically first with a small and thin artist's paint brush.

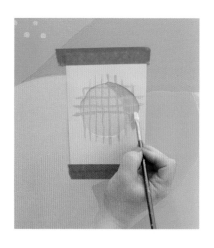

Repeat this step but this time going in a horizontal direction.

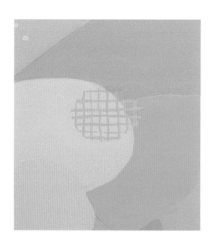

Peel back the stencil to reveal the pattern.

Top Tip

You can also use bought stencils for an interesting pattern.

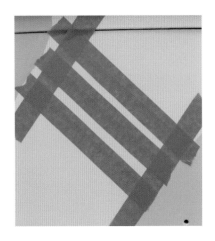

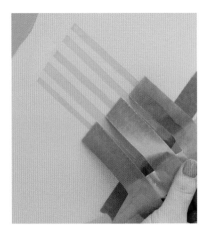

For a striped line look, use FrogTape to lay out a few lines in a row. Paint the first row of lines with Satinwood paint, peel back FrogTape and leave to fully dry.

To create thinner lines, I created a second layer of lines by sticking tape in the middle of the first set of lines. Then paint in the second row.

Peel back the FrogTape to reveal the striped lines. Leave to fully dry.

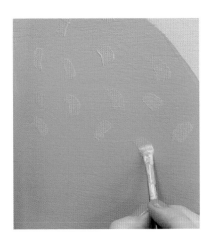

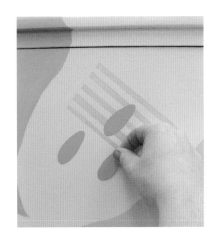

To create a confetti style pattern, use a small flat artist's brush to paint small lines in different directions in a section.

This is a simple step, but really effective. Place the decals from www.madeofsundays.com onto the piece and rub onto the timber to make sure they stay in place.

Choose a spot that won't get a lot of wear and tear so that they don't wear off.

Hello sign from www.tinythings.ie | Cake from www.kellylou.com | Disco ball tumblers from www.myshiningarmour.com

#furniturecrush

I CAN'T STOP THINKING ABOUT YOU

Stencilling and creating the Chipped Look

TECHNIQUE

Weathered Wardrobe With A Twist

STENCILLING AND CREATING THE CHIPPED LOOK

I love it when a piece of furniture tells a story and this method will do just that. The "weathered" look makes you think about the piece's past life and where it might have been used. This project can get a little messy, but that's where the fun is.

BEFORE

MATERIALS REQUIRED

Primer and three small jars
Sand paper
Satinwood paint (I used Colourtrend satin in
Milk Teeth, Andes Sky,
 Wildflower Boutique and Happy Face)
Vaseline and a paint scraper
Stencil (I purchased mine from www.stencilit.com)
Kid's round paint brush
Artist brush, spare cloths/rags and FrogTape

WARDROBES DON'T HAVE TO BE LIMITED TO THE BEDROOM AS THEY CAN MAKE GREAT STORAGE FOR COATS AND JACKETS IN THE HALLWAY.

Plan

Go Bold and different inside!

Chippy Chappy

Layer up colours

Play with colours on stencil

Real Weathered look

Use Paint colours on Underneath Distressed.

to tassel or not to tassel? that is the question

92

Method

Start by giving the surface a really good sand down. Remove all dust from the surface with a hoover.

On the first layer before priming, apply Vaseline to the paint scraper and scrape it on to the areas where you would like the wood-chipped distressed look to come through. For this piece, I concentrated on the edges of the wardrobe in small sections where I thought it might wear.

Lay out your three jars. Fill each one with primer until three-quarters full. Then fill the last quarter of each jar with the Satinwood paint in three different shades (in this case Andes Sky, Wildflower Boutique and Happy Face) and mix well.

Paint the wardrobe in sections using one of the primer shades. Don't worry about it being neat or overlapping as this will be covered up in a later step.

Paint the primer mix with all three colours onto the wardrobe in patches. The areas with Vaseline will appear to have a really uneven finish, but will be removed later.

When the primer is fully dry, use a paint scraper to apply the second layer of Vaseline in other areas that you would like the colours to come through.

Apply two coats of Satinwood paint for your overall colour. For this project, I used Milk Teeth. You will notice the areas where the Vaseline is applied as they will be uneven.

Once fully dry, apply the stencil. I decided to stencil in the panel areas. It depends on your surface, but a stencil works better on a flatter surface. Secure the stencil in place with FrogTape.

I decided to use a few different colours with the one stencil, but you can use just one. With the kid's paint brush, dab the first colour area with Satinwood paint.

It's important to dab rather than use strokes, as otherwise the hairs on the brush can slip underneath the stencil, causing an uneven pattern.

Continue with all the colours until you have completed the stencil section, making sure to hold the stencil steady with your spare hand.

Peel off your stencil to reveal the pattern underneath. Move the stencil onto the next section.

Once dry, any areas that need to be tidied up can be done so with a small artist's brush.

Here is the messy fun part: it is now time to remove the Vaseline with the paint scraper.

Note: There will be a small area on this patterned stencil where it overlaps to keep you on track. (If not, there are usually small points in each corner of the stencil to act as your guide, unless it is just a single design stencil.)

Drag the scraper horizontally around the whole piece, wiping the scraper in an old rag as you work your way around.

Repeat the last step, this time working vertically and again as you work your way around, wipe the residue with an old rag. Buff the whole wardrobe with a cloth.

I added some new handles and on the inside used a bold colour and some wallpaper from www.pipstudio.com, using high performance wallpaper adhesive and the same steps as project two.

THIS TECHNIQUE IS JUST AS EFFECTIVE USING ONE COLOUR. YOU CAN GO NEUTRAL OR BOLD.

Lights from www.cableandcotton.com | Handmade teddy from www.daintydressdiaries.com |Heart Pinata from www.hippenings.com | Inside Dutch painter wallpaper in red from www.pipstudio.com

Chocolate biscuits from www.thehappymail.co.uk

Everyone is

going to

LOVE you!

#furniturecrush

Colour Blocking & Gold Leaf

TECHNIQUE

The Ultimate Colour Crush

COLOUR BLOCKING AND GOLD LEAF TECHNIQUE

Colour blocking is a really good way to highlight detail in a piece in the most fun way possible. A steady hand is needed. Gold leaf detailing along the edge of the piece also adds an element of luxury and value.

BEFORE

YOU CAN PULL ELEMENTS OF COLOUR FROM AROUND YOUR ROOM AND INTRODUCE THEM IN ANOTHER WAY WITH THIS TECHNIQUE.

Plan

Pull vibrant colours for a POP

Gold leaf

you look good!

Paint handles

Pop in vibrant colours blocking areas for impact

light grey to let colours pop

MATERIALS REQUIRED

Satinwood paint
(I used Colourtrend satin in Winter's Breath, Milk Teeth, French Mustard, Wildflower Boutique,
Andes Sky, Pink Explosion)
Artist brushes
Gold leaf
Gold leaf glue
Sealer
Baby powder
Dry brush

101

Method

After painting the larger overall areas (Winter's Breath and Milk Teeth) it is now time to get ready for colour blocking. Break down the sections of your plan. Think of it as painting by numbers.

Planning your colour blocking is key, so a quick sketch will help you stay focused on your design and make it easier to follow.

Block in each colour section from your plan. I work colour by colour. Each piece will need two coats.

Keeping your hand steady, complete your colour blocking using the artist's brushes for control and precision.

Apply a thin layer of gold leaf glue, section by section, along the edge of the piece, about 10cm at a time. I use a small, flat artist's brush to keep control of the glue. The gold leaf will stick anywhere you place the glue, so applying a thin layer will ensure the glue doesn't dribble and will keep your gold leaf in a nice neat line.

Leave the glue to dry for around five minutes until the watery glue texture turns tacky.

After coating your hands with baby powder, carefully remove the gold leaf paper and apply to the glued section.

Pat the gold leaf paper with a dry brush and pull away the gold leaf paper for the next section.

Brush afterwards with the dry brush to remove any remnants of gold leaf paper.

Seal with a clear furniture wax or with a waterbased clear, non yellowing varnish.

Top Tip

Coating your hands in baby powder will make the fragile gold leaf paper a little easier to handle and prevent it from sticking to your hands.

Pavlova by Sharon Hearne Smith. Props and styling helped by Sharon. www.sharonhearnesmith.com

Your true colours are the most beautiful part of you.

#furniturecrush

Applying Fabric

TECHNIQUE

Cabinet Meeting

ADDING FABRIC

A cabinet is one of the easiest pieces of furniture to get your hands on and can come in all different shapes and sizes. In the past, they were mainly used to display china.

BEFORE

THERE IS GREAT BEAUTY IN REPURPOSING THEM, BE IT FOR CRAFT STORAGE, SHOE DISPLAY, IN YOUR BATHROOM OR AS A BOOKCASE.

Plan

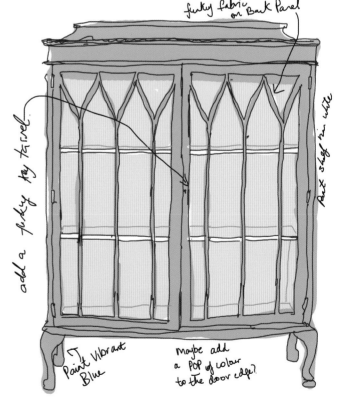

funky fabric on Back Panel

Paint shelf in white

add a funky tea towel

Paint Vibrant Blue

maybe add a POP of colour to the door edge?

MATERIALS REQUIRED

Undercoat
Satinwood paint:
(I used Colourtrend Milk Teeth on the inside and Enchanted Evening on the outside)
Small flat artist brush
Blade
Glass cleaner
Mod Podge glue (for fabric)
Scissors
Tack nails and a hammer

Method

The first thing you need to do is take out the shelves. Be careful, as sometimes when the shelves are removed and the door of the cabinet is wide open, the piece can fall forward. Once the shelves are removed, you will need to take out the back panel.

The best way is to work from the inside by carefully and gently hammering the back panel gradually from corner to corner. The back panel will begin to push away from the cabinet.

Once the back panel begins to get really loose, gently remove it, along with any old nails or staples carefully with a pliers.

Remove the old paper or fabric from the back panel. Gently sand the back panel to remove any old glue residue.

When painting the areas around the glass, you can tape and paper off the glass to protect it. Use a small, flat painter's brush to get into any of the timber edging on the glass panels. When the paint is fully dry, you can remove any paint on the glass with a blade, then clean the glass inside and out.

Clean the panel and undercoat. Even though the board will be covered in fabric, undercoating the back panel will help block out any timber peeping through, as the glue can tend to make some fabrics look transparent. It will also flag any stains that may need to be sealed before applying the fabric.

Once your panel is cleaned and undercoated, apply the fabric. You can also use wallpaper like in project two.

 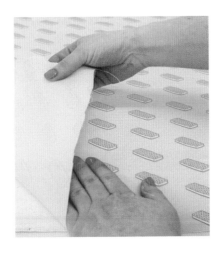 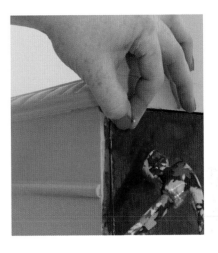

Lay the panel out flat and lay the fabric on top. Cut around the fabric to the approximate size of the panel. This will remove any excess fabric that may get in your way during this process, but make sure to allow for some wiggle room.

Once you have the fabric cut, paint the back panel quickly with the glue, giving the whole panel an even coat.

Place the fabric flat on top of the panel and with the palm of your hand, flatten it onto the board. If there is a bubble in the centre, you can pull back the fabric and push out the air bubble.

Work your way all around the panel. Once you have the fabric in place, cut around the edge with a scissors and remove any extra fabric. Leave to fully dry.

Place the panel back into the cabinet. You may need an extra pair of hands to help you keep the panel in place. With small tack nails, hammer the tack around the edge of the cabinet keeping it in place, making sure it slots back into position properly. When you have the panel in place, you can paint it with a layer of primer, undercoat and paint.

Top Tip

I often find when I am working with cabinets that I can get "bleed through" while applying the undercoat. If this happens, use Colourtrend's Prime 2, and look at Troubleshooting on page 122.

Posters (W,O,W) from www.madeofsundays.com| eat more cake banner from www.nikkimcwilliams.com|
light box from www.myshiningarmour.com

Transferring font

TECHNIQUE

Fantastic Font

TRANSFERRING FONT TECNHIQUE

This is one of my favourite techniques because the possibilities are endless. I discovered this method by accident when I was writing a receipt and transferred onto the table top I was writing on by mistake. A happy mistake. I have been using this method ever since. Writing bureaus are rare to come across, but I love the character and practicality of a bureau.

BEFORE

YOU CAN TRANSFER ANY FONT OR GRAPHIC THAT YOU WISH AND IT COULDN'T BE EASIER.

Plan

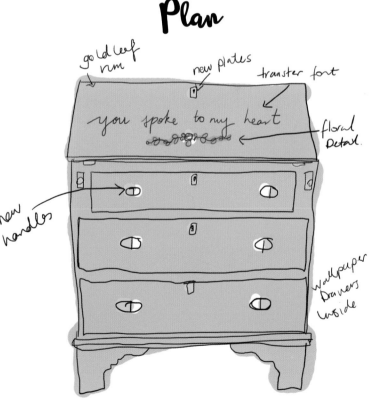

gold leaf rim

new plates

transfer font

you spoke to my heart

floral Detail.

new handles

wallpaper Drawers inside

MATERIALS REQUIRED

Satinwood paint
I used Colourtrend satin (Blue Folly and Beag)
Carbon paper
Pencil
Gold leaf
Frog tape
Thin artist's brush
Template from
www.kylelane.ie/booktemplate

Method

Once fully dry, tape your template onto the piece of furniture where you would like it positioned. You can download the one I made for this project by going to www.kylelane.ie/booktemplate

Place the carbon paper under your template, with the darker side facing down, and tape it in place.

Trace over all the details on your template with a sharp pencil or pen. Peel back the template and the carbon paper.

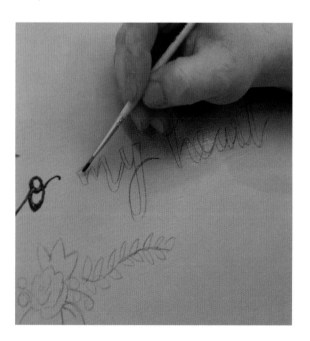

You are now left with the outline of your template. Use Satinwood paint to fill in the lines using a thin artist's brush.

For the flower detail, break down the paint into layer blocks, painting the large centre flower a deep pink first, followed by the two side flowers in mustard and the berries in white.

Start adding in the small details in between the flowers, like stems and leaves (check the template if you are unclear).

When this layer is fully dry, you can begin adding the small details that are just delicate brush strokes. Follow the template for the position of these lines if you cannot fully see the first layer of paint.

When the paint was fully dry, I added a drop shadow using gold paint (template available on www.kylelane.ie/booktemplate)

Ceramic Vases, circular prints and bird brooch from www.perdozendesign.ie

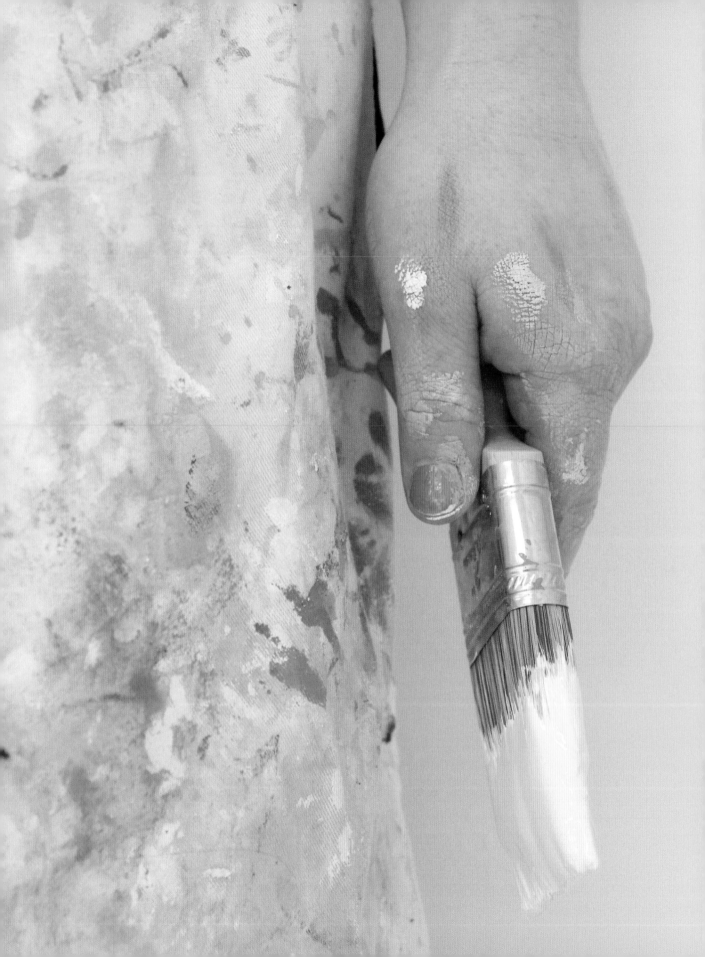

Still want more?

The Painter's Club is an online paint membership group to learn more painted furniture techniques each month.

Share your work with others, get advice and keep learning.

To join the community go to www.kylelane.ie/paintersclub

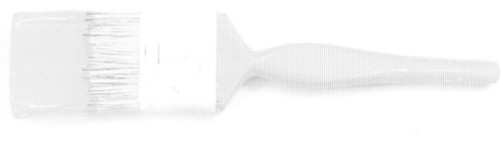

The Painter's Club

STAIN SPOTS OR BLEED-THROUGH STAINS

These are red or pink blotches that come up on your piece at your preparation stage. If a stain is not blocked, it will continue to come through. I always use a coat of Colourtrend's Prime 2 Epoxy . This is a water-based primer that acts like a shellac primer without the strong smell and covers over the stain or bleed.

WOODWORM

This is a pesky little problem and it needs to be treated straight away. It appears like small little spots on a piece, so if you are buying second hand furniture, make sure to always look out for this problem. It can be treated with chemicals and there are lots of different products on the market for this. If your piece has woodworm, remove it from your home and treat it as soon as possible. Make sure that you are treating the whole piece and not just the hole, which is where the woodworm has come out. The best way to explain it is to picture the piece of furniture as a sponge that needs to soak up all the woodworm killer. Follow the manufacturer's instructions very closely.

RIPPING PAPER

If you are tidying up the edges of paper and it begins to rip, it is a sign that your blade might be beginning to blunt, so continue instead with a fresh blade.

PAPER BUBBLING

This can be a real pain if it is the final touch on a piece of furniture. If you're noticing air bubbles on your papered area, you may not have allowed enough time for the glue to soak in, or you may not have worked the air out with the palm of your hand properly. If it is just one big bubble that you can't push out, try making a tiny cut in the paper with a blade and push out the air there. Once you add a tiny bit of paste, you don't notice the little cut area.

BLEEDING TAPE LINES

If you have a bleeding line on the edge of your tape, you may be using the wrong tape. FrogTape is the only job for this. If this happens when you are already using FrogTape, your brush may have been recently washed and loaded with water. Make sure your brush is dry before painting.

STICKY SURFACE

If your surface feels really sticky and is drying very slowly, you may not have left adequate drying time in between coats. Leave to fully dry (overnight) and sand back the surface with a fine sandpaper to get it smooth again before putting on a final coat.

PAINTING A WAXED SURFACE

No paint, primer or undercoat will adhere to a surface if there is a wax barrier. You must remove the wax before you prepare the piece. If you try and remove the wax with a sander, it will quickly clog up your sander and you will just be wasting sandpaper. You can remove the wax with white spirits, making sure you are in a well ventilated area wearing a mask and gloves.

BAD SMELLS

Sometimes that old musty smell is difficult to get out of that chest of drawers you bought and I have just the trick. Put cat litter into the drawers and close them for seven full days, allowing the cat litter to soak up the odour. You may need to repeat if it's a stubborn smell.

Frequently asked questions

Can I skip the priming/undercoat step?
Never skip this step, no matter what kind of paint you're using.

Can I paint with water-based paints over oil-based paints?
You will need to prepare the surface first, sanding and using a primer. The water-based paints tend not to adhere to the oil-based surface properly.

Can I paint over laminate?
You can pretty much paint over any surface with the right primer. To paint over a laminate surface, sand with a medium sandpaper and prime, then paint the surface like normal.

Is it ok to paint in the sun?
In Ireland we don't get much of an opportunity, but in the summer months, it's ok to paint in the shade and then let the furniture dry in the sun. If you are in a really hot country or if there is a serious heatwave, the high temperature may bubble the paint and undo all your hard work.

Can I paint with test pots?
Paint in test pots is usually for the wall, unless there is a specific test pot for wood.

Paint brush or roller?
I use a paint brush for awkward areas and then I would use a paint roller on a large area.

Can I paint over a painted surface?
Yes you can. You can either strip it back with paint stripper or you can sand the surface smooth with a fine sandpaper, prime and work from there.

What kind of paint would I use to paint outdoor furniture?
With Colourtrend's satin paint, you can paint interior or exterior wood and metal, and one litre will last you for lots of projects. With other paints, just check the manufacturer's instructions on the back of the tin.

Can you paint PVC?
Yes you can paint your PVC windows and door any colour you like. Just make sure you have the correct primer to adhere to the surface (i.e. Colourtrend Prime 2) and paint with satin.

Share Your
Furniture Crush Projects

I would love to see what you get up to after reading this book.

If you have tried any of the techniques, just tag your projects
#furniturecrush on your social media and I'll find them.

#furniturecrush

Acknowledgements

I have been thinking about this book for years and I remember the very day I decided that I was going to find a way to make it happen. And it never would have if it wasn't without…

To my editor Maria Moynihan, who always supported and encouraged me, made me feel like I wasn't doing this alone, calmed me and helped me break it all down. I don't think I could have managed this without you. You are a total legend.

I would like to thank my family for all their support. To the main man, my biggest crush, my husband Vinny. You have always been so supportive of my ideas and dreams and have been a constant reminder that of course I can do it, no matter what. For helping me grow and believing that everything will work out and leaving me paint and change our home, more often than you would like, I love the bones of you.

To my mother who always told me I could do whatever I dreamed about if I worked at it, and continuously supporting me. To my dad for teaching me not only a good work ethic, but little tips and tricks for getting the best finishes, helping me to grow by thinking outside the box and problem solve, which is invaluable. To all my crazy siblings, nieces and nephew who give constant encouragement and are always up for the banter.

To all the funders, who took a chance on my dream, for funding, sharing and being so patient.

To the www.fundit.ie team to helping me through my crowdfunding, for being always positive and so approachable. Thank you Andrew, Orla, Claire, Jackie, Helen and Michelle.

To my friends who constantly supported me throughout my crowdfunding journey:
Susan O'Reilly, Annmarie Williams, Jackie O'Flynn, Helen Fenton and a special, massive thanks to Laura O'Connor and Shannon Forrest (you two really pushed me through). To my soul sister, Catherine Keher, thank you for all your support and encouragement, for listening to every idea, thought and rant I had. Let's be honest Catherine, that's never going to stop, book or no book.

To all the other businesses who got behind me. Thank you Sharon Hearne Smith www.sharonhearnesmith.com for the beautiful pavlova and helping me style the ultimate colour crush project, and Kelly from www.kellylou.com for the amazing cake in the happy hour project. Nicola from Blush beauty www.blush.ie for the gorgeous geometric nails on hand model Jyll Power, thanks Jyll.

For support close to home, special thanks to Miss Ellie's Takeaway, Irishtown, Clonmel; Martin's Fruit and Veg, Irishtown, Clonmel; Martins Tiles and Bathrooms; Bob Fitzgerald's hardware; Fieldmaster Clonmel, Tipp FM, The Bookmarket, Clonmel and Pat Cleere's Clonmel.

Huge thanks also to

Nikki from www.myshiningarmour.com/ie/
Laura from www.hippenings.com
Catherine from www.daintydressdiaries.com
Elaine from Brookwood pottery www.brookwoodpottery.com
Catherine Keher from Per Dozen Designs www.perdozendesigns.ie
Maura from www.themessybrunette.com
Aisling from www.thesmallbusinessfairy.com
Joanne and Caroline from www.gaffinteriors.ie
Ali from www.purposehub.ie
Joanne Mooneyfrom www.tinythings.ie

Thanks also to Lily O'Brien's, Chia Bia seeds and a special thanks to Colourtrend paints.

For business friends away from home,
Alba, Gemma and Thomas from www.madeofsundays.com
Gwen from www.gwennieslab.nl
Nikki from https://nikkimcwilliams.com
and Tina from www.thehappymail.co.uk